THE

Archive Photographs

SERIES

ARMSTRONG WHITWORTH
AIRCRAFT

Armstrong Whitworth Argosy Men, a cartoon by the famous Chris Wren, showing many of the leading personalities that were involved in the Argosy project. It was drawn for use in the special feature on the Argosy that appeared in the 16 January 1959 issue of *The Aeroplane*.

THE
Archive Photographs
SERIES

ARMSTRONG WHITWORTH
AIRCRAFT

Compiled by
Ray Williams

CHALFORD

First published 1998
Copyright © Ray Williams, 1998

The Chalford Publishing Company
St Mary's Mill, Chalford,
Stroud, Gloucestershire, GL6 8NX

ISBN 0 7524 1060 1

Typesetting and origination by
The Chalford Publishing Company
Printed in Great Britain by
Bailey Print, Dursley, Gloucestershire

Assembly line of BE2c aircraft at Gosforth early in 1915. The fuselage of the single seat FK1, with the later form of tailplane and elevators, can be seen in the left foreground.

Contents

The Farman biplane used by the Avro Flying School at Brooklands in 1911. The repair of this particular aircraft was Armstrong Whitworth's first venture into aviation.

Acknowledgements

The Armstrong Whitworth Aircraft Company, like most other aircraft companies, went through a period of contraction and mergers before Bitteswell, the last of the old AWA sites, was closed in the mid 1980s. During this period much valuable historical material was lost and what survived was generally saved by interested individuals.

In recent years the excellent Midland Air Museum at Baginton in Coventry has taken on the role of collector and guardian of AWA's history, along with other more general aircraft-related material. The enthusiastic team who run the Coventry Branch of the Rolls Royce Heritage Trust, currently housed at the Rolls Royce factory at Mickleover, near Derby, is responsible for preserving the heritage of Armstrong Siddeley Motors. It is also pleasing to note that the Armstrong Whitworth, Newcastle upon Tyne collection is preserved as part of the Vickers PLC Archive at the Cambridge University Library.

During my research of the Sir W.G. Armstrong Whitworth Aircraft Company over many years, I have received help from many people to whom I extend my sincere thanks. These include John Austin, the late Bert Butler, the late Bill Else, Eric Franklin, Jimmy Morrow, Alec Scott, Joe Staite, Fred Sanders, Alan Troughton and Albert Whitehouse - all ex AWA personnel, and Ron Frost, ex ASM, who has helped with photographs from the RR Heritage Trust archive. Also Jack Bruce who helped with the First World War period, allowing me to use photographs from the superb J.M. Bruce/G.S. Leslie Collection, and my good friends Eric Harlin and George Jenks for their continuing support over rather more years than I wish to remember. I must also particularly record my gratitude to Dick Teasdale, who has put in much time and effort in searching for information relating to some of the more obscure photographs that are used in the book. Last, but by no means least, I am extremely grateful to Richard Riding, the editor of *Aeroplane Monthly*, for permission to use the superb Chris Wren cartoon *Armstrong Whitworth Argosy Men* that originally appeared in *The Aeroplane* in January 1959.

Ray Williams
Lymm,
March 1998

Introduction

Armstrong Whitworth was an old and famous name on Tyneside. The origin and development of this great engineering firm was due almost entirely to the efforts of one man, W.G. Armstrong, who although a solicitor by profession, had an intense interest in mechanical engineering.

In 1847 he opened a small works at the village of Elswick upon Tyne, employing between 20 and 30 men. Stimulated by his inventive genius, the company prospered and rapidly expanded. His initial products were hydraulic machinery, cranes and, during the Crimean War, mobile artillery. It was particularly for his work on guns that Armstrong was knighted in 1859 and by the time he had been created a baron in 1887, his engineering empire had been extended to include two shipyards, one adjacent to the Elswick works for warships and the other at Walker on Tyne for merchant ships.

A contemporary of Armstrong was the Stockport-born Joseph Whitworth, who is probably best remembered for his work on standard screw threads. His Manchester-based tool making business started in 1833 and soon earned a reputation for the high quality of the machine tools they produced. Whitworth, who was knighted in 1869, found himself in direct competition with Armstrong when he also became involved in the manufacture of artillery pieces. It was presumably this duplication of activity that was to result in the amalgamation of the Armstrong and Whitworth companies into the Sir W.G. Armstrong Whitworth and Company Limited (AW) during 1897, some ten years after the death of Sir Joseph.

AW's first venture into the aviation field came about in 1911 when repairs were carried out on a Farman biplane and its Gnome engine after it had crashed at Blaydon Racecourse, near Newcastle. The Farman was later sold to A.V. Roe & Co. Ltd who used it at their Brooklands flying school during the latter part of that year. Despite this initial involvement, AW showed no immediate interest in further aircraft work. Diversification of Armstrong Whitworth's activities continued when, in 1912, they reached an agreement with the All British Engine Company Limited (ABC) to manufacture ABC aero-engines. The arrangement was that AW was to produce two engines for the Government engine competition to be held in 1914, and a batch of 100 hp engines, all designed by Granville Bradshaw of ABC. However in the event, neither type of engine proved satisfactory and in mid 1914 AW cancelled their contract with ABC. Some two years later AW, in collaboration with Harry Ricardo, an engine designer, made another attempt to get into the aero-engine business, but at that time the commercial prospects did not appear good so they again abandoned the project.

In 1913 the War Office placed orders with the firm for a small number of BE2a biplanes. This resulted in Armstrong Whitworth establishing an aerial department in a company-owned sawmill at Scotswood in August 1913, with Captain I. Fairbairn-Crawford as general manager. The first AW built BE2a was completed in April 1914 and shortly afterwards a larger order was received by the company for BE2bs.

With this increase in business the aerial department had to expand and it was transferred to a disused skating rink at Town Moor, Gosforth. In addition, the services of Frederick Koolhoven, the famous Dutch aircraft designer, were acquired as chief designer. Prior to this he had been employed by the British Deperdussin Company where he had played a major part in the design of their fast racing machines.

Koolhoven soon completed his first design for Armstrong Whitworth, an orthodox single seat biplane powered by a 50 hp Gnome engine and identified as the FK1. Shortly after war was declared in 1914 the designer managed to convince the Admiralty that he could improve the performance of its Bristol TB8 aircraft by fitting redesigned wings. As a result, one of the three machines with the RNAS was released for modification, but there was no significant improvement and no further machines were altered.

Towards the end of 1914, two batches of BE2cs were ordered by the War Office and as these orders progressed, Koolhoven once again managed to convince the authorities that if left to design an aeroplane to the same specification, he could produce a simpler machine with an improved performance. The result of these deliberations was the FK2/FK3 series which was ordered in quantity by the War Office, mainly for training purposes.

In 1915, H.H. Golightly, working directly for Fairbairn-Crawford, was appointed manager of a new airship department at Barlow. Set up at the request of the Admiralty, work was immediately put in hand to manufacture Submarine Scout (S.S.) non-rigid airships for the Royal Navy and a programme of rigid airship production was also started. It is understood that a total of six rigid airships were ordered, although in the event only three were completed. Of the three, R.25, R.29 and R.33, the first two proved to be rather unsatisfactory, but R.33, a copy of the German Zeppelin L.33, was probably the most successful of all the British rigid airships.

Although prototypes of several Armstrong Whitworth designs were produced, the only other aircraft to be put into large scale production was the FK8 corps reconnaissance aeroplane, 751 being built by Armstrong Whitworth at Gosforth and at least a further 838 aircraft being completed by sub-contractor Angus Sanderson and Co., also of Newcastle upon Tyne.

When production of the FK8 ceased at Gosforth in the spring of 1918, its place on the production line was taken by the Bristol F2B fighter which remained in production until November 1918.

When Koolhoven left Armstrong Whitworth in 1917 to join the BAT Co. as chief designer, his place was taken by Frank Murphy, who was destined to have only two of his designs built by the company. Both aircraft were single seat fighters, the FM4 Armadillo and the Ara. The Armadillo was apparently designed primarily as an exercise to check the capabilities of AW's design department. The Ara was a more serious attempt to produce a fighter but was unsuccessful because like many of its contemporaries, it was rendered ineffective by the failure of its powerplant, the ABC Dragonfly engine.

The Ara proved to be the last Armstrong Whitworth aircraft built at Newcastle. Because of the reduction of work following the Armistice the company decided in September 1919 to close the aerial department at Newcastle and Barlow and leave car, aircraft and engine work to their recently acquired Siddeley Deasy Company in Coventry. Like many of the armament companies following the First World War, the Sir W.G. Armstrong Whitworth Company ran into serious financial difficulties which continued until the major part of the firm was taken over by the Vickers Company in 1928, becoming Vickers Armstrong Limited.

John Davenport Siddeley, born in 1866, was the dominant force in the Siddeley Deasy and later Armstrong Siddeley organisation until his retirement in 1936. He was knighted in 1932 and raised to the peerage as Baron Kenilworth of Kenilworth in 1937; he died in 1953.

To follow the later developments of the company it is necessary to go back to 1915. At this time, in parallel with Armstrong Whitworth's venture into aviation, the Siddeley Deasy Motor Car Company of Coventry was also becoming involved in aviation, starting with a contract to produce 90 hp RAF 1a aero-engines. Eventually, in 1916, the company became involved with aircraft production when it received a production order for RE7s.

The driving force behind the Siddeley Deasy organisation was their managing director, John Davenport Siddeley. Born in 1866, Siddeley began his engineering career in the drawing office of the Humber Cycle Company during 1892. After about a year with them he moved on to the Pneumatic Tyre Company, later to become part of Dunlop. Having gained experience of the tyre industry he set up the Clipper Tyre Company in Coventry during 1898, but during the next three years he developed a considerable interest in the motor car. This led him to resign his position as managing director of the Clipper Tyre Company in 1901 to establish a company to import Peugeot cars from France. He appears to have done this mainly to obtain experience of the rapidly developing automobile industry and early in 1902, he formed the Siddeley Autocar Company to manufacture cars. At a motor show held in the Crystal Palace early in 1903 he was able to exhibit a range of four models. It was no doubt due to the success of this venture that the Vickers-owned Wolseley Tool and Motor Car Company, with the agreement of Siddeley, took over the Siddeley Autocar Company in 1905. Siddeley was initially employed as their sales manager and then appointed general manager the following year.

Almost from the outset, Siddeley's relationship with the main Vickers Board was far

A view inside the Siddeley Deasy factory in Coventry showing completed late production RE8 fuselages awaiting transfer to Radford Aerodrome for final assembly, flight test and delivery.

from harmonious and when he heard of the resignation of Captain H.H.P. Deasy as managing director of the Deasy Motor Car Manufacturing Company in 1908, he saw a possible escape route. Consequently, early in 1909 he applied for the position of general manager of the Deasy Company and when successful, resigned his position at Wolseley. His appointment was an instant success and within a few months the Deasy Board promoted him to managing director. Under Siddeley's control the company soon earned an enviable reputation as a manufacturer of high class motor cars and in November 1912, it changed its name to the Siddeley Deasy Motor Car Company.

Following the declaration of war in August 1914 the existing production at Siddeley Deasy rapidly ran down and the Parkside works soon became involved in the manufacture of military vehicles. In 1915 the company branched out into aero-engine production, initially manufacturing the 90 hp 8-cylinder RAF 1a engine designed by the Royal Aircraft Factory, Farnborough. The RAF 1a was superseded in production by the 150 hp RAF 4a and then, in 1916, a Beardmore-Halford-Pullinger (BHP) engine was redesigned at Parkside to emerge as the Siddeley Puma.

Aircraft production started in 1916 with a production order for the RE7 and 100 were built before production was switched to the RE8, of which 1,024 were built. Finally, in 1918, there was an order for 150 of the twin engine de Havilland DH10a Amiens bombers, but only a small number of aircraft had been completed when the contract was cancelled shortly after the end of the war.

As the war progressed the Royal Aircraft Factory at Farnborough came in for a great deal of criticism for inefficiency, leading to questions being asked in Parliament. This resulted in the Government setting up a committee of enquiry under the chairmanship of Sir Richard Burbidge in 1917. The report of the Burbidge Committee, which the Government accepted, recommended that the Royal Aircraft Factory should not continue with the design and construction of aeroplanes and aero-engines but should become an aeronautical research establishment. These changes made a number of design and production staff surplus to requirement and Siddeley managed to recruit several of them, including Captain F.M. Green (later to be promoted to major) as chief engineer, S.D. Heron, an engine design engineer and John Lloyd as chief of aeroplane design. Green and Heron, along with Siddeley's existing engine designer F.R. Smith, were immediately involved with the development and production of the Puma engine. The first project for John Lloyd's aircraft design department was the RT1, an improved version of the RE8, and this was followed by two original designs, the SR2 Siskin fighter and the Sinaia bomber.

By the end of the war John Siddeley was virtually in total control of the company. However Siddeley Deasy, like many other firms, was suffering from the sudden move from war to peace. Although it was a difficult time Siddeley decided that the company, having built up a high level of expertise, should continue with the design and manufacture of aero-engines and aircraft. To protect it through this very difficult post war period Siddeley decided that the company should amalgamate with a suitable engineering business and in 1918, negotiations were opened with the Daimler Company. These negotiations soon ended in failure and before the end of 1918, Siddeley turned his attention to the Sir W.G. Armstrong Whitworth and Company Limited of Newcastle upon Tyne. Armstrong Whitworth was a company that Siddeley had done business with during the war which had impressed him with the quality of their workmanship. The negotiations were successful and in February 1919 Armstrong Whitworth paid some £420,000 for all the shares of the Siddeley Deasy Company.

In May 1919 Armstrong Whitworth set up a subsidiary company known as the Sir W.G. Armstrong Whitworth Development Company to control their Siddeley Deasy acquisitions. Before the end of the year the Development Company had formed a Coventry-based subsidiary known as Armstrong Siddeley Motors Limited (ASM), with John Siddeley as managing director, to take over all Armstrong Whitworth's and Siddeley Deasy's automobile and aviation activities.

In July 1920 the aircraft side of the business was set up as a separate business under the title of Sir W.G. Armstrong Whitworth Aircraft Company Limited (AWA). Whitley Abbey Aerodrome was purchased in 1920 to replace Radford Aerodrome, which had been used for test flying the Siddeley Deasy built aeroplanes. Aircraft production however, remained at the Parkside works until it was transferred to Whitley in 1923, although the aircraft design department remained at Parkside until 1930.

One of the first projects undertaken by the this department under its new AWA banner was a carrier-borne fleet reconnaissance aircraft for the Royal Navy. The contract stipulated that the aircraft was to be a conversion of the DH9A, of which large numbers of surplus airframes were available from wartime production. The resulting aircraft, the Armstrong Whitworth Tadpole - a particularly ugly aeroplane - was evaluated by the Royal Aircraft Establishment at Farnborough, but the production order was placed with Westland for their equally ugly Walrus.

One of the earliest activities to take place at Whitley was the formation of a flying school with Major J.C. Griffiths as chief flying instructor and aerodrome manager. This venture proved quite successful and in 1923 it received a Government contract to train RAF reserve pilots, when it became the Sir W.G. Armstrong Whitworth Reserve Flying School. The school continued to prosper and in 1931 was formed into a separate company known as Air Service Training Ltd (AST), wholly owned by the Development Company, and transferred to the old Avro aerodrome at Hamble. The

The first Siddeley RT1 B6625 showing the SE5 type radiator and engine cowling for the 200 hp Hispano Suiza engine. The RT1, an improved variant of the RE8, was the first project undertaken by John Lloyd after his arrival at Siddeley Deasy, and the first to be built under the Siddeley banner.

chairman of AST, Air Marshal Sir John Higgins, was also, at the time, the chairman of AWA.

It was company policy when the flying school was at Whitley, for the flying instructors to undertake any routine test flying that became necessary. However, from 1919 until the end of 1925, most experimental flying and all maiden flights of new types were undertaken by the famous freelance test pilot, Capt Frank Courtney. In 1923 Capt J.L.N. Bennett-Baggs joined the company as a flying instructor and became the chief flying instructor when Major Griffiths was killed test flying a Siskin III in 1924. Soon afterwards, Bennett-Baggs was joined by Alan C. Campbell-Orde and Douglas A. Hughes, who was unfortunately killed in a crash during 1927. Bennett-Baggs, after becoming a demonstration pilot and performing liaison duties for the company with the RAF, finally left to join Blackburn Aircraft in 1932.

By 1928 Campbell-Orde had become, in effect, the chief test pilot, a position he held until he joined British Airways in the autumn of 1936. He was followed in the same role by Charles K. Turner-Hughes, who held the position throughout the hectic wartime period, retiring from the company in 1946.

During the early '20s, development of steel construction was undertaken by Green and Lloyd with assistance from Major H. Wylie, a consultant structural engineer. Their work resulted in the redesign of the Siskin to introduce all-steel construction. In this form the Siskin was ordered in quantity for the RAF.

Production of Siskins began to build up during 1924 and with the order for Siskin Vs for Romania, in addition to the RAF contracts for Siskin IIIs, a total of 71 Siskins were completed in 1925. The prototype Atlas and Ajax also made their maiden flights during the same year. The Siskin was the mainstay of production at AWA until 1928 when it was overtaken by the Atlas. In 1926 three Ape aerodynamic research aeroplanes were completed for the RAE, Farnborough and three Argosy Mk.1 airliners were delivered to Imperial Airways.

The prototype Starling, a planned replacement for the Siskin, made its first flight in 1927. It proved however, to be a failure and an improved version, the AW16, was produced in 1930. Although no orders were forthcoming from the Air Ministry, 17 of these aircraft were sold in China during the early '30s, together with 14 Atlas IIs.

Although by 1925 the Armstrong Whitworth Development Company in Coventry was prospering with the build up in production of the Jaguar engine and Siskin, the parent company in Newcastle was suffering extreme difficulties with the decline of the heavy engineering and ship-building industries. John Siddeley was obviously most unhappy about 'his' companies in Coventry propping-up the parent company. To solve this he decided to purchase the Development Company, which he succeeded in doing in December 1926. The name of the company was subsequently changed in 1927 to the Armstrong Siddeley Development Company.

In 1928 Siddeley purchased A.V. Roe and Co. Ltd from the Crossley Motors group. His reason for acquiring it is reputed to have been to help maintain the market for Armstrong Siddeley engines, although the opportunity to expand his empire for what must have been a bargain price of about £250,000 must have helped him to make the decision. Also in 1928, the Development Company was further expanded when it took over one of its suppliers, High Duty Alloys Ltd, after it had run into financial difficulties.

The same year was significant for AWA with the installation of its first wind tunnel at Whitley, a low speed tunnel designed by William Farren (later Sir William) who was a lecturer at the Imperial College of Science and Technology in South Kensington.

During 1929 production of the Siskin at Whitley came to an end, although production continued at several sub-contractors until 1930. AWA remained busy, with Atlas production superseding the Siskin and the final batch of four Argosies being built for Imperial Airways. The completion of the Atlas contracts and the slow build up of Hawker Hart production in 1932 created a rather lean period for the firm, but this improved in 1935 with the expansion of Hart production and the placing of a production contract for the AW38 Whitley bomber. The Whitley was to remain the mainstay of AWA production until it was superseded by the Avro Lancaster during 1943, by which time 1,814 Whitleys had been produced.

Work was started in the early 1930s on the design and development of a manually operated, balanced gun turret which was put into production for use on Whitleys and Ansons. Unfortunately they proved to be inadequate under wartime conditions and were generally replaced by power driven turrets.

The Amstrong Siddeley Development Company joined with Hawker Aircraft Ltd in 1935 to form the Hawker Siddeley Aircraft Company. Although Sir John Siddeley (he had been knighted in 1932) did not join the board of the new company he remained as chairman of the Development Company until he finally retired in June 1936. Siddeley, who was raised to the peerage in 1937 as Lord Kenilworth, died in 1953.

It had become obvious by 1935 that both the factory and aerodrome at Whitley were inadequate for the quantity production of large aeroplanes. It was decided to build a factory at Coventry's municipal aerodrome at Baginton and the production of Whitleys started there in 1936, before the factory had even been finished. With the RAF expansion plan, AWA's commitments were such that it proved necessary to transfer production of the Ensign for Imperial Airways, to Air Service Training at Hamble. This was followed later by the sub-contracting of the Albemarle to A.W. Hawksley Ltd, a new company set up by Hawker Siddeley in the shadow factory at Brockworth.

With the start of the Second World War, Armstrong Whitworth took control of factories at Leicester, Nuneaton, Northampton, Sywell and Bitteswell and by the end of 1943, some 60 separate units were in use providing a total of some 2,000,000 sq ft of floor space. It was during this period that AWA built up their excellent production organisation and for this much of the credit must go to H.M. Woodhams, the general manager, and S.W.D. Lockwood, the works manager. Woodhams was appointed chairman and managing director in 1950, being succeeded on his retirement in 1960 by Lockwood. Lloyd had recruited Lockwood for his design team in 1919 and he had moved from design to become assistant works manager in 1921. Woodhams joined the company in 1923 as chief inspector, having in 1919 gained the distinction of having obtained the first Air Ministry ground engineer's licence for aero-engines. In 1935 he was appointed works manager and two years later became general manager.

In 1944 Armstrong Whitworth took over the management of Short's Swindon factory at the behest of the Ministry Aircraft Production. Consequently the final 108 Short Stirling bombers built at Swindon were, at least in theory, built by AWA.

AWA's factory at Whitley Abbey Aerodrome in 1928 with the general purpose Atlas I G-EBNI in the foreground.

One of AWA's more unusual tasks was the furnishing of the C.45 Skymaster, EW999, that had been presented by President Roosevelt to Winston Churchill early in 1944. Included in the layout was a conference room, panelled in walnut, containing a walnut-finished table to seat eight people. A stateroom was provided for Churchill equipped with a divan, wardrobe, writing desk and easy chairs. The passenger compartment was equipped to carry ten people. The aircraft, completed in October 1944, was delivered to Northolt in November to be inspected by Churchill. EW999 was only in service for a short while as it was returned to the USA immediately after the Socialist victory in the first post war general election.

A similar task was undertaken in 1947 when two Avro Tudor 3 aircraft, G-AIYA and G-AJKC, were fitted out as VIP transports for use by cabinet ministers. Serial numbers VP301 and VP312 were allocated. However, when virtually complete, the requirement was cancelled and the two aircraft were returned to A.V. Roe at the end of 1947, still bearing their civil registrations.

When the war ended in 1945, the large contracts for Lancasters and Lincolns were severely curtailed, resulting in AWA vacating all their dispersal factories and stopping production work at their Whitley factory which was turned into a store. The wind tunnel however, remained at Whitley until it was moved to Baginton in 1948. In the early post war period the Government made use of some of this spare production capacity by placing contracts with AWA for the manufacture of sections of prefabricated aluminium houses. Even so, the work force of 12,000 in 1944 was reduced

The two prototype AW38 Whitleys K4586 and K4587 under construction. These aircraft, designed to meet Air Ministry specification B.3/34 for a night bomber, made their maiden flights at Whitley on 17 March 1936 and 23 December 1936 respectively with AWA's chief test pilot A.C. Campbell-Orde at the controls.

to 3,000 by the end of 1946. Production, supplemented by refurbishing and conversion work on Lancasters and Lincolns, was to provide the company's main work load until 1950. During the Berlin Airlift in 1948, AWA serviced 86 Avro Yorks on a short turn-round basis to maintain adequate numbers of aircraft in service over that critical period.

Immediately after the war AWA started a programme of basic guided weapon research that led to a contract in 1946 for the manufacture of liquid-propellant rocket motors for the RTV1 missile that was being developed by the RAE at Farnborough. After this the company, in conjunction with the Guided Projectiles Establishment at Westcott, started work on an experimental missile which was subsequently developed into the Sea Slug, a ship-to-air guided missile.

AWA's missile work expanded rapidly and was soon putting great pressure on the resources available at Baginton, so in 1948 it was decided to transfer this work to Whitley. Walter Lockwood, the works director, had the responsibility for the conversion of the factory into what was probably the finest missile research and production unit in the United Kingdom. In 1952 he was also responsible for opening AWA's Australian division which controlled the trial facilities at the Woomera Rocket Range.

The slow speed wind tunnel was returned to Whitley in 1952 and over the next few years a further four wind tunnels were installed, providing wind tunnels ranging from the original 1928 slow speed tunnel to a supersonic tunnel providing a speed of up to Mach 3.

HMS *Girdle Ness* firing a Sea Slug Mk.1 during successful trials in the Mediterranean. The Sea Slug was the Royal Navy's first operational ship to air guided missile.

R.F. Midgeley was appointed chief test pilot when Turner-Hughes retired in 1946. Unfortunately a back injury received in a motor accident forced him to retire in 1948. He was succeeded by Eric G. Franklin, who remained as chief test pilot at Coventry until the closure of the Baginton factory in 1965 when he transferred to Hawker Siddeley Aviation Limited at Woodford Aerodrome.

Early in the war, John Lloyd became involved in research into laminar flow and boundary layer control. A section of wing was produced for the National Physical Laboratory in 1942 and this was followed by a set of laminar flow wings that were flown on Hurricane II, Z3687. Research was continued with the AW52G flying wing glider and later with the AW52 turbojet powered flying wing aircraft. Tests on these aircraft proved that it was impossible to maintain the standard of surface finish required and the research programme was dropped during the early 1950s.

Immediately after the war AWA, with their AW55 Apollo airliner, attempted to break into the civil market. Although two prototypes were built the aircraft did not enter production, having been rejected in favour of what was to become one of Britain's most successful airliners, the Vickers Viscount.

As production of Lincolns began to reduce in 1949, a batch of Meteor F Mk.4s was sub-contracted from the Gloster Aircraft Company. This was followed by large orders for the Meteor F Mk.8. During this same period, AWA was given the task of designing and developing a night fighter variant of the Meteor. The first version was the Meteor NF Mk.11 which was followed in production by the NF Mk.12, NF Mk.13 and finally, the NF Mk.14. The night fighters proved very successful and in addition to large numbers being produced for the RAF, a small quantity were exported for use by the air forces of six other countries. The Meteor NF Mk.11 was also developed into a target tug for the Royal Navy and identified as the Meteor TT Mk.20. Between 1957 and 1965, 24 aircraft were converted by AWA, in addition to a quantity converted by the Royal Navy.

Development and production of the Hawker Sea Hawk was handed over to AWA in 1952 and the same year, the Hawker Hunter was put into production. The final type to be sub-contracted to AWA was the Gloster Javelin which entered production in 1955. When the final AWA built Javelin was delivered during 1958, a total of 4,035 aeroplanes designed by other companies had been built by AWA at Coventry.

John Lloyd was appointed technical director in 1948 and was succeeded as chief designer by H.M. Watson, who was in turn succeeded by E.D. Keen in 1955. Keen, who proved to be AWA's last chief designer, was responsible for the design of the AW650/660 Argosy.

Unfortunately the Argosy did not prove to be a great success as the demand for a specialist freighter aircraft at that time was considerably less than anticipated and a total of only 16 AW650 Argosies were sold to civilian operators, and three of the second batch of ten aircraft were never completed. The military variant, the AW660 Argosy C.Mk.1, was more successful with a total of 56 being built for the RAF.

The steady decline of the aircraft industry continued throughout the 1950s and in 1961 the Gloster Aircraft Company was merged with Sir W.G. Armstrong Whitworth Aircraft Co. Ltd to form Whitworth Gloster Aircraft Ltd; then in 1963 this new company merged with A.V. Roe Co. Ltd to become the Avro Whitworth Division of Hawker Siddeley Aviation Ltd. The prospects for the division looked very good in 1963 when contracts were placed for the design and development of the AW681 (later HS681) STOL military transport as a replacement for the RAF's Beverley and Hastings aircraft. Unfortunately, early in 1965 the newly elected Labour Government cancelled the HS681 along with most other contemporary aircraft projects, as an economy measure. This had a devastating effect on the Coventry part of the division, bringing about the closure of the factory at Baginton and reducing Bitteswell, the sole surviving part of the AWA empire, into a service and maintenance unit.

At the same time Hawker Siddeley decided to disband the divisional organisation and with it, the individual division identities were abandoned, leaving all the factories to operate as Hawker Siddeley Aviation Ltd.

Following the closure of Baginton, the factory and aerodrome at Bitteswell were kept busy with programmes for the refurbishment and modification of Gnats and Vulcans for the RAF and Hunters for resale to various foreign air forces. Bitteswell was also responsible for the conversion of 12 maritime reconnaissance Shackletons to the airborne early warning role. In 1973 work started on the conversion of 14 Argosy C.Mk.1s into navigation trainers, designated the Argosy T.Mk.2, as a replacement for the Vickers Varsities operated by No.6 Flying Training School at RAF Finningley. However just before the first aircraft was completed early in 1975, it was announced that the conversion programme had been cancelled, another victim of defence spending cuts. Sadly the workload continued to decline and in the mid 1980s the site was closed and sold for commercial development.

A visit by members of the Hawker Siddeley main board to Bitteswell during October 1958 with Sir Roy Dobson, the managing director of HSA, in earnest discussion with Herbert M. Woodhams, the chairman and managing director of AWA. Eric G. Franklin, the chief test pilot and E.D. Keen, the chief designer, are contemplating the complexities of the Argosy centre control console. Behind them can be seen Sir Thomas Sopwith, with his back to the camera, and Sir Frank Spriggs.

One
Newcastle upon Tyne

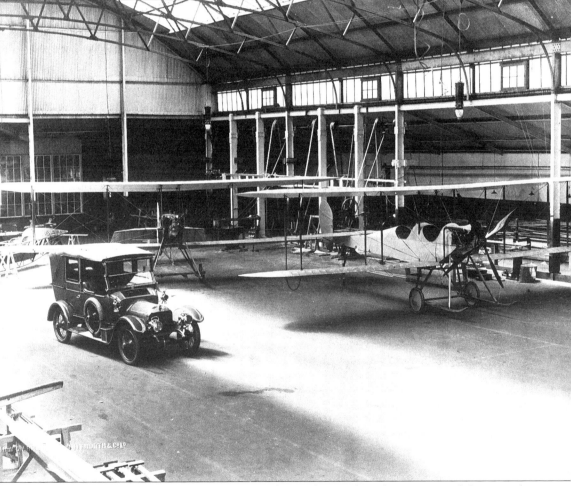

Assembly of BE2a aircraft in the Armstrong Whitworth aircraft works, a converted skating rink at Gosforth, in May 1914. The car is an Armstrong Whitworth Lauderette and to the left is the airship gondola built for HMA No. 2.

The Armstrong Whitworth FK1, designed by the Dutchman Frederick Koolhoven, was a rather fragile looking single seat scout powered by a 50 hp Gnome rotary engine, which made its first appearance in September 1914.

The fifth production FK2 No. 5332 with a 70 hp Renault engine and the early form of fin and rudder. The FK2 was designed by Koolhoven to basically meet the same operational requirements as the BE2c but to be much easier to build.

A standard production AW FK3, B9572, built under sub-contract by Hewlett and Blondeau. Of the 494 FK3s that were built, only 43 are believed to have been built by AW. The FK3 - known by most in the RFC as 'Little Ack' - saw the radical and very sensible change of putting the pilot in the front cockpit and the observer in the rear.

A close up of an AW built airship car, with its 100 hp Green engine, before fitting to the envelope. The airship car was developed from the FK2 fuselage and is understood to have been identified as the FK4.

An S.S. non-rigid airship with an AW airship car, being manoeuvered on the ground. The cylindrical gravity fuel tanks which distinguish the type can be seen above the cockpits and gave the airship an endurance of about 12 hours.

The rather bizarre AW FK5 triplane was designed as a three-seater anti-airship fighter, powered by a 250 hp Rolls Royce Eagle engine. The two gunners were each provided with a 0.303 inch Lewis machine gun and were accommodated in the nacelles mounted on the middle wing and projecting forward of the engine. It is understood that this aircraft never flew because the general manager, Captain Fairbairn-Crawford, considered it to be unsafe.

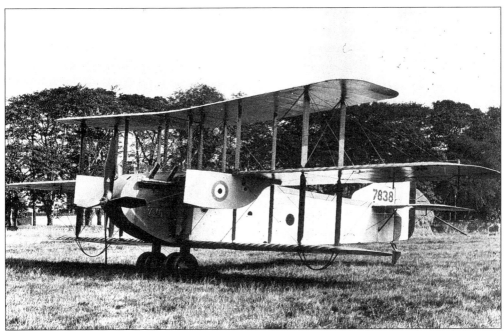

When in 1916 the Royal Flying Corps issued a requirement for a long range escort and anti-airship fighter, Koolhoven produced a redesign of the FK5. Although four of this new design, the FK6, were ordered, only the first, No. 7838, was built. The project was soon abandoned when it was found to have a disappointing performance although more importantly, gun-synchronising gear had been developed which enabled the use of more conventional aircraft with guns firing through the propeller disc for this role.

The first production FK8, A2683, at Duke's Moor in August 1916. Powered by the 160 hp Beardmore engine, it had an improved performance over its predecessor the FK3.

A standard production FK8, B230, in France during January 1918. Although the FK8 was only marginally larger than the FK3, it became known in the service as 'Big Ack', presumably to differentiate it from the FK3. Part of the Constantinesco gun-synchronising gear may be seen just below and behind the propeller. The exhaust stack projecting over the upper wing was to eliminate hot gases distorting the pilot's view.

One of the experimental FK8s, B214, fitted with a 200 hp RAF 4d engine, at the RAE, Farnborough, in July 1917.

The first AW quadruplane fighter, the FK9, made its first appearance in 1916 and was sent to the Central Flying School for trials in November 1916.

This is possibly the first FK10 quadruplane after the original 110 hp Le Rhone rotary engine had been replaced by a 130 hp Clerget engine and a fairing had been fitted over the pilot's Vickers gun. The FK10 varied from the FK9 primarily with the introduction of a deeper fuselage and modified tail surfaces. In the background can be seen the 150 hp Lorraine Dietrich powered FK8.

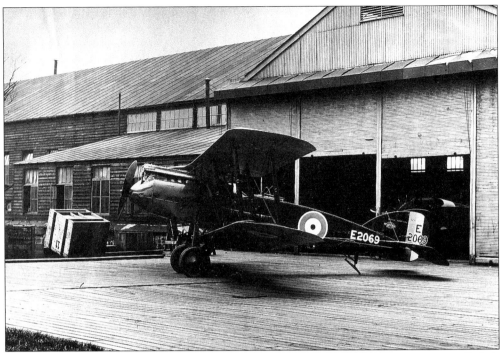

An AW built Bristol F2B fighter, E2069, powered by a 240 hp Siddeley Puma engine at Duke's Moor in 1919. Contracts for the production of 550 Bristol fighters were placed with AW but only 169 are known to have been completed.

The 230 hp Bentley BR2 powered FM4 Armadillo X-19 was the first aircraft designed by AW's new chief designer, Frank Murphy, following Koolhoven's departure from the company. The Armadillo, built as a private venture, was heavily criticised by an RAF pilot Captain A.D. Allen, who flew it in May 1918, and although it made a few flights afterwards the project was soon abandoned.

The first Ara, F4971, at Duke's Moor in January 1919. The Ara had a good performance but was marred by the unreliability of the 320 hp ABC Dragonfly engine. Although three Aras were built, development was short-lived as the aircraft was abandoned when the aircraft department at AW's was closed late in 1919.

His Majesty's Airship (HMA) R.25 was built by AW for the Admiralty to a design by Vickers. It was AW's first rigid airship and was built at the new airship factory at Barlow in Yorkshire. The R.25, which was launched on 14 October 1917, was 535 ft long with a diameter of 53 ft. R.25 was not successful and was withdrawn from use in November 1918 after accumulating a total of only 220 flying hours.

AW's second rigid airship, the R.29, was basically a redesign by the Admiralty of the R.25. HMA R.29 proved to be a considerable improvement and was the only British rigid airship to see action, dropping bombs on the German submarine UB-115 on 29 September 1918.

The third rigid airship built by AW at Barlow, moored at Croydon Airport in 1921. It was a copy of the captured German Zeppelin L.33 and proved to be the best of the AW built airships. This airship was considerably larger than the two previous ones, being 644 ft long with a diameter of 79 ft. Although built for the Admiralty, R.33 was transferred to the Air Ministry in 1920 and the following year acquired the civil registration G-FAAG. It was scrapped at Cardington in 1928.

Two
Coventry –
the Early Years

RE8 No. A3433 was one of the first batch of RE8s built by Siddeley Deasy powered by the 140 hp RAF 4a engine. In this aircraft the pilot occupied the front cockpit with the observer in the rear. Although powered by the same engine as the later RE7s built by AWA, the RE8 had a better performance, being a little more refined and nearly 400 lb lighter.

A standard production RE8, E43, at Radford Aerodrome, the aerodrome used by Siddeley Deasy for all their test flying. The RE8 was the mainstay of Siddeley Deasy aircraft production during the First World War with 1,024 being built.

The second RT1, B6626, powered by an 140 hp RAF 4a engine. Although six were ordered (B6625 to B6630) it is believed that only the first three were completed, as it was considered that the RT1 did not show sufficient improvement over the RE8.

A Siddeley Deasy built DH10A Amiens E7845 of 216 Squadron, being wheeled out of the hangar in Heliopolis, Egypt, in 1921.

The first Siddeley SR2 Siskin C4541 at Radford Aerodrome in the spring of 1919. Although based on the proposed Royal Aircraft Factory SE7, the Siskin was the first aircraft to be designed and built by Siddeley Deasy. Six Siskins were initially ordered but only three are known to have been completed and they were all initially powered by ABC Dragonfly engines.

C4541 at Whitley after it had been fitted with an early version of the Armstrong Siddeley Jaguar engine. Flight trials of the Siskin had shown the airframe to be satisfactory whilst the Dragonfly engine proved to have faults so serious that development and production was cancelled. The Siskins were then re-engined with the new Jaguar engine, a combination that proved to be a great success.

The Siddeley Sinaia J6858, the third and final aircraft project to be designed and built by the Siddeley Deasy company at the RAE, Farnborough, on 23 June 1921, two days before its first flight. The Sinaia, powered by two 500 hp liquid cooled Siddeley Tiger engines, was a long distance general purpose and bombing aeroplane that failed to progress beyond the prototype stage.

Three
Between the Wars

One of the two Siskin IIs, without any markings but believed to be G-EBHY on display at the Armstrong Siddeley stand at the International Aviation Exhibition (ILUG 23) held in Gothenburg, Sweden from 20 July until 3 August 1923. The Siskin II differed from the original Siskin mainly by the introduction of a fuselage constructed of steel tube rather than of wood. The first Siskin II, G-EBEU, built as a two seater, was completed in mid 1922. Flown by Frank Courtney it took part in the 1922 King's Cup Air Race but had to withdraw at Manchester with a broken centre section fitting. The following year after conversion into a single seater, G-EBEU, again flown by Courtney was successful in winning the race.

J6583, the Siskin III prototype, was the first to be built with an all-steel structure, a method of construction that had been developed by AWA to meet the Air Ministry requirement that all future aircraft for the RAF had to be of steel construction.

The fifth production Siskin III, J6999, at the RAE, Farnborough, in February 1924, where it was being used for experiments with wireless transmissions.

Siskin III J7155 of No. 111 Squadron based at Duxford. No. 111 was the second squadron to be equipped with the type, receiving its aircraft in June 1924, some six months after No. 41 Squadron had started to receive theirs.

G-EBJQ was a conversion by AWA of the first production Siskin III, J6981. The main change was the introduction of the additional fuel tanks under the upper wings. The conversion, along with that of G-EBJS, was carried out specifically for the 1924 King's Cup Air Race. Although G-EBJS, flown by Frank Courtney, had to withdraw from the race with engine trouble, G-EBLQ flown by Flight Lieutenant H.W.G. Jones managed to finish in fourth place.

J7000, Siskin IIIDC (dual control) was originally completed as a conventional single seat Siskin III before being converted by AWA into the first two seat trainer version during 1924, Siskin IIIDC J7552 of No. 111 Squadron. In addition to the Siskin IIIDCs used by the RAF training units, each operational Siskin squadron had at least one on their strength.

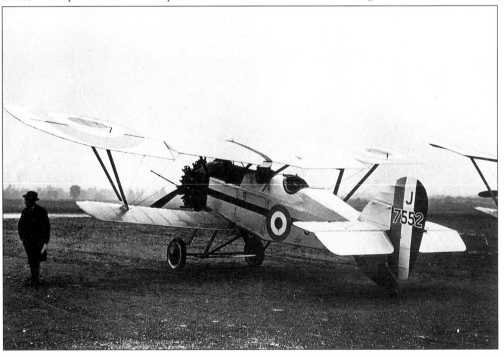

The last production Siskin IIIDC, G-ABHU, was built for the AWA Reserve Flying School in 1930 and was to remain in service with the school and its successor, Air Service Training Ltd at Hamble, until the end of 1937.

The prototype Siskin IIIA at the A&AEE Martlesham Heath where it appeared without any identification except national markings. Built as a private venture it differed from the Siskin III primarily in having a deepened fuselage, a strengthened structure and the replacement of the under-fin with a simple tail-skid. The Air Ministry took the aircraft over towards the end of 1926 when it allocated serial number J8428.

Siskin IIIA, J9900, of No. 41(F) Squadron being started with a Hucks Starter at Sutton Bridge in 1930. J9900 was one of 84 Siskin IIIAs built by the Bristol Aeroplane Company. Siskin IIIAs were also built under sub-contract by Blackburn, Gloster and Vickers.

A line-up of Siskin IIIAs of No. 29 Squadron with those of No. 43 Squadron in the background.

Siskin IIIB, J8627, was an attempt to extend the life of the RAF Siskin IIIAs by offering the Air Ministry the alternative of upgrading the existing RAF fleet rather than buying a totally new replacement.

The sole Siskin IV, G-EBLL, showing the return to the wide chord lower wing after the narrow one used for the RAF variants. This aircraft came second in the 1925 King's Cup Air Race, flown by Squadron Leader H.W.G. Jones.

Siskin V No. 2 of the Romanian order made its first flight on 22 October 1924. The Romanian contract was for 65 aircraft and although 33 had been flown when the contract was cancelled in 1925, none had been delivered.

The flight shed at Whitley in 1924 when production of Siskin Vs for Romania was well under way; in the background can be seen Siskin IIIs for the RAF and a solitary Wolf.

Siskin V, G-EBLQ, won the 1925 King's Cup Air Race flown by the Imperial Airways pilot Captain F.L. Barnard. This aircraft crashed at Whitley on 19 July 1926 killing AWA test pilot Douglas A. Hughes.

Siskin V, G-EBLN, shortly before the start of the 1925 King's Cup Air Race with J.L.N. Bennett-Baggs (his foot on a chock) and F.T. Courtney standing in front. Bennett-Baggs flew G-EBLN and Courtney the Ajax G-EBLM; both failed to complete the race, ending up in the same ditch at Newcastle.

The AW Tadpole, J6585, at the RAE, Farnborough, on 26 August 1920. The Tadpole was AWA's first project, a conversion of a DH9A, E8522, into a three seat fleet reconnaissance aircraft for the Royal Navy. Only the prototype was built, as the production contract was placed with Westland for 36 of their Walrus aircraft.

The second Wolf, J6922, at the RAE, Farnborough, in March 1924 where it was used for photographic experiments. Designed and built as a corps reconnaissance aircraft, three prototypes were ordered by the Air Ministry. No production orders were to follow and after evaluation the prototypes were used for experimental purposes.

Three Wolf aircraft were built to Air Ministry Specification 8/22 for an advanced trainer to be used by the AWA Reserve Flying School. G-EBHJ, shown here at Whitley, the second of these civil registered aircraft, flew for the first time on 16 August 1923. The first two aircraft were flown in 1923 whilst the third, G-AAIY, which was ordered much later, was not delivered until 1929.

G-EBHI after a landing accident at Whitley; apparently the Wolf had a reputation for this type of accident. Even so the Wolf remained in service with the Flying School until it was transferred to Hamble in 1931, when they were withdrawn from service. Air Service Training, the successor to the AWA Reserve Flying School, retained the last Wolf, G-AAIY, for several years as a ground instructional airframe.

The Awana troop transport was AWA's first original design to be built under the new company name. It is shown here shortly after being rolled out at Whitley in 1923 bearing serial number J6860. This number was already being carried, correctly, by the Awana's competitor, the first Vickers Victoria which was already well into its flight test programme. The Awana flew for the first time on 28 June 1923 shortly before the serial number was changed to J6897.

The second Awana, J8698, at the RAE, Farnborough, on 27 March 1924. No further Awanas were built as Vickers were awarded the production contract for their Victoria.

The first prototype AW Atlas I Army Co-operation (AC) aeroplane, G-EBLK, was built as a private venture at Whitley from where it made its first flight on 10 May 1925 in the hands of Captain Frank T. Courtney. The Armstrong Siddeley Jaguar III powered Atlas was designed to meet Air Ministry specification 30/24 for a replacement for the AC version of the Bristol F2B fighter.

Atlas I, G-EBNI, during a demonstration tour by AWA test pilot J.L.N. Bennett-Baggs to Greece in 1928. G-EBNI was an Atlas I general purpose aeroplane built as a private venture and used by the company until it was bought by the Air Ministry and allotted serial number J9129.

Atlas I AC, J9983, of No. 4 Squadron with message pick-up hook extended.

Atlas I AC, J9971, of 'B' Flight No. 208 (AC) Squadron over Heliopolis in July 1933. During the 1930s the squadron was carrying out anti-slavery patrols in the Middle East. This aircraft has been fitted with an aerodynamically balanced rudder with no fin that became standard on later Atlas Is.

Atlas I AC, 409, of No. 22(AC) Squadron, Royal Canadian Air Force. This aircraft is a refurbished former RAF Atlas, K1531, that was supplied to Canada in October 1936.

A flight of three Atlas I ACs of the Greek Naval Air Service. Two Atlases were supplied to Greece by AWA and a further ten were built under licence by the Greek National Aircraft Company.

Atlas I AC, J9998, at Calshot in 1931, when it was used as a hack by the RAF's High Speed Flight during the Schneider Trophy Competition. The aircraft was fitted with experimental stainless steel floats that had been designed and built by AWA.

Atlas J8802, the first of two Atlas day bombers built for the Air Ministry. After extensive trials, including some by Nos. 5 and 27 Squadrons in India, it was decided that the Atlas was unsuitable for the bombing role. The main external feature of the Atlas day bomber was the additional fuel tanks mounted under the upper wing centre section.

The first prototype dual control Atlas I Trainer, J8792, was the conversion of a standard AC aircraft to meet Air Ministry Specification 8/31, photographed here during trials at the A&AEE, Martlesham Heath.

Six Atlas Trainers under construction at the Whitley factory.

Six Atlas Trainers awaiting delivery on the airfield at Whitley in 1930. K1177 and KII87 were destined for the RAF College, Cranwell, whilst the remainder were to be packed for transportation to No. 4 Flying Training School at Aboukir, Egypt. To the left of the aircraft can be seen the SE5A, G-EBIB.

The dual control Atlas G-ABHX, one of a batch of three Atlases delivered to the AWA Reserve Flying School at Whitley in April 1931 for advanced training. A total of four Atlas Trainers were supplied to the school which subsequently became Air Service Training Ltd after moving to Hamble at the end of 1931. All four Atlases continued to give good service until they were withdrawn in 1938.

G-EBYF, originally built as an Atlas AC, in 1928 for use by AWA as a demonstrator. It is shown here after conversion into the Atlas II prototype. The main changes are new aerodynamically improved wings and a supercharged AS Panther III engine fitted with a Townend ring.

The first production Atlas II, A-3, was subsequently put on the British Civil Register as G-ABIV. It is shown here about to take-off from Whitley for a demonstration tour of the Baltic States in November 1931 with Alan C. Campbell-Orde at the controls and an engineer, Robert (Bob) Hunter, in the rear cockpit. The increased fin area and increased depth of the rear fuselage were introduced to improve spin recovery.

One of a batch of 15 Atlas IIs in Hong Kong before delivery to the Kwangsi Air Force in China.

Atlas II G-ABIV in its fully developed form in 1934, fitted with an AS Tiger IV engine driving a four-bladed propeller. The fuselage is skinned with light alloy and a new longer undercarriage is fitted.

Ajax G-EBLM, a general purpose aircraft, was designed and built in parallel with the Atlas I and flew for the first time in mid 1925. It was structurally similar to the Atlas with the only significant difference being the design of the observer's cockpit. The general purpose Atlas G-EBNI and the two day bombers, J8802 and J8803, sometimes appear in the records as Ajaxes, but are listed in AWA's Constructors Number Register as Atlases.

Ajax G-EBLM was purchased by the Air Ministry in 1927, receiving serial number J9128. After being refurbished and modified by AWA at Whitley it was delivered to the RAE, Farnborough, in April 1928. The photograph shows it at the RAE in May 1928 with leading edge slots fitted to the upper wings, a geared Jaguar VI engine and larger cockpit apertures.

The first Argosy I, G-EBLF, in the early Imperial Airways colour scheme of dark blue and silver. The number 15 on the nose was applied for its participation as a new type at the RAF Pageant, Hendon, on 3 July 1926. Designed specifically for Imperial Airways' Middle East routes the Argosy was a large three-bay biplane powered by three 385 hp Armstrong Siddeley Jaguar III engines. It was capable of carrying 20 passengers for up to 330 miles at a cruising speed of 90 mph. G-EBLF flew for the first time at Whitley on 16 March 1926 with Captain F.L. Barnard, an Imperial Airways pilot, at the controls.

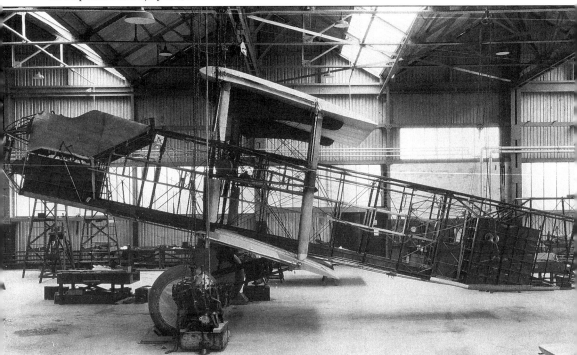

An Argosy - probably the first - under construction at Whitley. The dark boxes in the nose and rear are luggage compartments.

Argosy I, G-EBLF *City of Glasgow*, flying over Croydon after it had been repainted in the later Imperial Airways' colour scheme of silver with royal blue lettering and trim. Imperial Airways named each of their Argosies after a famous city. On 1 May 1927, G-EBLF was used to inaugurate the luxury Silver Wing service between London and Paris.

Four Argosy IIs were built for Imperial Airways. These saw the introduction of the 420 hp Jaguar IVA engine, streamlined engine nacelles and large vertical servo tabs fitted to the trailing edge of the lower mainplane. The photograph shows the second Argosy II, G-AACI *City of Liverpool* at Croydon alongside one of Air Union's Bleriot 165s in Golden Ray livery. G-AACI was lost in one of the worst air disasters of its era when it crashed in Belgium killing all 15 passengers and crew.

The last surviving Argosy II, G-AACJ, at Stanley Park, Blackpool, in 1936. In 1935 it was bought by United Airways who, after installing additional seats and windows in place of the rear luggage compartment, used the aircraft for pleasure flights around Blackpool Tower. In January 1936 it was taken over by British Airways and was withdrawn from use later in the year.

The second AW Ape, J7754. The Ape was designed to meet Air Ministry specification 48/22 for a two-seater aerodynamic research aeroplane. Three Apes, J7753 to J7755, all initially powered by the AS Lynx, were built for the Aerodynamic Flight at the RAE, Farnborough.

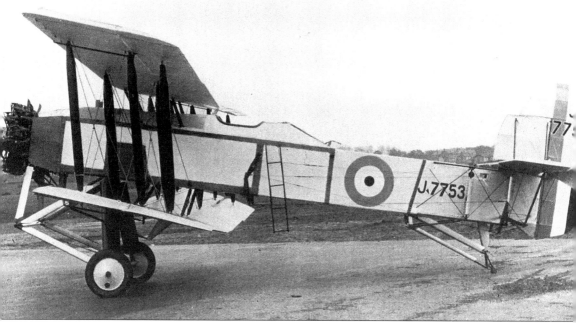

The first Ape, J7753, after being fitted with an AS Jaguar engine. To counteract the increased engine weight the rear fuselage can be seen to have been extended. J7753 remained in use until early 1930 when it was written off in a flying accident.

The AW14 Starling day and night fighter was the first aircraft to be given an AWA project number in addition to a name and was intended as the successor to the highly successful Siskin. The first Starling, J8027, powered by the 425 hp Jaguar engine, was found to have very dangerous stalling characteristics which were resolved by changing the aerofoil section of the wings. J8027 was subsequently purchased by AWA who registered it as G-AACH and used it as a demonstrator.

The second Starling, a Mark II, J8028, was built as a zone fighter and had a generally improved appearance from the original along with a larger upper mainplane and smaller lower. The changes delayed the completion of J8028 until November 1929, over two years after the first flight of the J8027.

Two additional Starling IIs were built as a private venture. The first with class 'B' registration, A1, was built as a fleet fighter and is seen here on a visit to the Royal Naval Air Station at Gosport. Note the Townend ring fitted to the engine that was a standard fit on both private venture Starlings.

Aries J9037 was built to Air Ministry specification 20/25 for a version of the Atlas I AC designed for easy maintenance. Large access panels were introduced in the side of the front fuselage to provide improved access to internal equipment, along with additional interplane struts to reduce the number of flying wires.

The prototype, AW15, made its maiden flight on 6 June 1932 flown by Alan C. Campbell-Orde. The photograph shows it on a test flight from Whitley in September 1932. G-ABPI, powered by four 340 hp Armstrong Siddeley Double Mongoose engines (subsequently known as the Serval) was named Atalanta by Imperial Airways, a name that was adopted as the type name for the entire fleet of eight AW15s. G-ABPI was the only AW15 that was fitted with fully faired wheel spats.

The wreckage of G-ABPI after it had crashed on take-off at Whitley on 20 October 1932 when all four engines cut-out. The pilot, Alan C. Campbell-Orde and the only passenger, the Chairman of AWA, Air Marshal Sir John Higgins, escaped virtually unhurt, but the co-pilot, Donald Salisbury Green, unfortunately received severe head injuries which brought his flying career to an end.

Atalanta G-ABTL *Astraea* was one of three African-based Atalantas that were transferred to India in 1938. In March 1940 G-ABTL was impressed into the Indian Air Force as DG450.

G-ABTM *Aurora* in its final guise as DG454 of the Indian Air Force, showing the additional windows fitted in the forward cargo doors for its reconnaissance role. It was lost when it made a forced landing in a swamp near Calcutta. A total of four Atalantas were operated by the Indian Air Force with the last two being withdrawn from service in June 1944.

The first AW16, S1591, a fleet fighter as originally rolled out at Whitley in December 1930. The AW16 was a major redesign of the Starling that impressed the Air Ministry enough to prompt them to order a prototype of the fleet fighter variant. S1591 was a conversion of the Starling II fleet fighter A1.

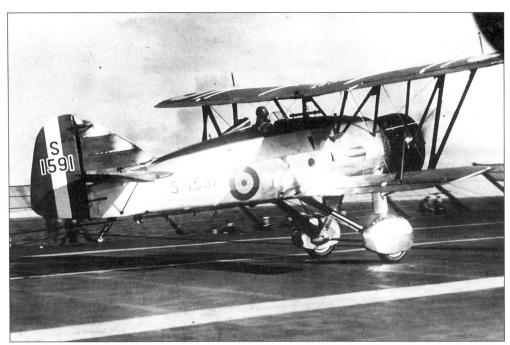

S1591 on *HMS Courageous* in September 1933 for trials by 800 Squadron Fleet Air Arm. The extended fin and the increased depth of the rear fuselage were introduced to improve its initially rather poor spin recovery characteristics.

The second AW16 A2 at Whitley, early in 1931, was a major conversion of the Starling II A2, which was carried out as a private venture.

Two AW16s at Hunjao Airfield, Shanghai, in May 1934 during their delivery from Hong Kong to Kaifeng for the Honan Provincial Government. A total of five AW16s were supplied to Honan, who subsequently presented them to the Chinese Central Government for the Chinese Air Force.

The company's AW16 demonstrator, G-ABKF, at Kjeller during a sales tour of Norway in October 1932. AWA's test pilot, Donald Salisbury Green, can be seen forward of the wing. John Siddeley loaned G-ABKF to Alan Cobham for his National Aviation Day Flying Displays in South Africa during the winter of 1932-33, where it was flown by Charles K. Turner-Hughes, who was later to become a test pilot with AWA.

G-ABKF at Whitley in March 1935, when it was being used as an engine test bed for Armstrong Siddeley's experimental 3-row 15-cylinder engine. The engine proved to be troublesome and offered little improvement on existing engines so development was abandoned.

The AW19, with its class 'B' registration A3, was a private venture general purpose, bombing and torpedo carrying aircraft designed to Air Ministry specification G.4/31. Campbell-Orde took A3 for its maiden flight at Whitley on 28 February 1934. The open cockpit forward of the upper wing provided an excellent field of vision for the pilot. The gunner's station was located aft of the wing and a cabin was provided between the two cockpits for navigation and bomb aiming.

During April 1935, A3 was purchased by the Air Ministry, allotted serial number K5606 and allocated to ASM for Tiger engine development. ASM continued to operate K5606 until November 1938 when it was quite badly damaged when turned over in a gale. It is shown here shortly after it had been damaged and before it was decided that it would not be cost effective to carry out repairs; it was finally struck off charge in June 1940.

An AWA built Hawker Hart day bomber, K3892, of No. 605 Squadron at Castle Bromwich in 1936.

AWA's last production Hawker Hart carrying the AWA class 'B' marking A4 was built as a private venture for the company and used for trials with an AS Panther engine during 1936.

The prototype AW23, shortly after it had been rolled-out at Whitley in May 1935, before its markings had been applied. Designed and built to Air Ministry specification C.26/31 for a bomber/transport, it made its maiden flight from Whitley on 4 June 1935 with Alan C. Campbell-Orde at the controls. The AW23 was AWA's first aircraft that had a retractable undercarriage.

An AW23 box spar in a structural test rig at Whitley. The AW23 was AWA's first aircraft to have a box spar, an innovation that was to feature in virtually all AWA's subsequent aircraft.

A demonstration of loading heavy freight into the AW23 at Whitley in 1935.

The prototype AW23, K3585, on an early flight in 1935. K3585 proved to be the only AW23 to be built, as its competitor the Bristol Bombay was selected for the RAF.

The first AW27 Ensign, G-ADSR, emerging from the flight shed at Air Service Training, Hamble, for initial engine runs. It made its maiden flight on 21 January 1938 in the hands of C.K. Turner-Hughes, AWA's chief test pilot, and was delivered to Imperial Airways on 5 October 1938.

The King's Flight Airspeed Envoy III G-AEXX taxying past Ensign G-ADSR during a visit to Baginton.

A line-up of five Ensigns at Baginton awaiting modification by AWA in 1939. Fourteen Ensigns were ordered for Imperial Airways, 12 were delivered by October 1939, with the last two being delayed until 1941 when they were completed as Wright Cyclone G.102A powered Ensign IIs.

The Indian registered VT-AJG *Euryalus* at Hamble in August 1939; the registration was replaced with G-ADTA shortly after its first flight. It was originally planned that four Ensigns were to be operated out of Calcutta on the Empire routes by the Indian Trans-Continental Airways. This arrangement was presumably cancelled because of the imminence of the war.

Ensign IIs G-ADSR *Ensign* and G-AFZU *Everest*. A total of eight of the first batch of Ensigns were converted to Mk.II standard by the installation of the 950 hp Wright Cyclone engines. G-AFZU was, in effect, the prototype Mk.II, being the first to fly with the Wright engines.

Ensign II, F-BAHO, photographed in Vichy, France. The final production Ensign II G-AFZV *Enterprise* made a forced landing on 3 February 1942 in French West Africa. After the crew had been rescued by a Sunderland of the RAF, the Ensign was abandoned. It was subsequently recovered by the French authorities in Africa who used it, registered as F-AFZV, for a short while before it was delivered to Vichy where it was registered as F-BAHO.

Ensign II, G-ADTB *Echo*, back in its original natural finish towards the end of the war. All the surviving Ensigns reverted to this scheme during what were their final C. of A. overhauls in 1944/45.

Four

The Second World War

Although six companies submitted projects to meet the Air Ministry Specification P.27/32 for a single engined day bombing aircraft, only prototypes of the AW29 and the Fairey Battle were ordered. This photograph shows K4299 shortly after it had been rolled out and while it was prevented from flying by the Air Ministry because they considered there was insufficient ground clearance for the elevator trailing edge.

A general view inside the Armstrong Siddeley engine installation department hangar at Baginton in mid 1939, showing the AW29 being stored after plans to convert it into an engine test bed for the 1,350 hp AS Deerhound engine had been abandoned. Also in the hangar are the AS Deerhound powered Whitley engine test bed, K7243, Whitley Mk.III K8966 that was being used for engine overheating trials, and the prototype Fairey G.4/31 K3905 used for AS Tiger engine development.

The AW35 Scimitar was the last of AWA's biplane fighters. G-ACCD was the first, a conversion of the penultimate AW16 that had been retained by the company as a demonstrator. Power was provided by a 568 hp fully supercharged AS Panther VII engine which was totally enclosed in a long chord cowling.

Three of the four Scimitars that had been bought for the Norwegian Army Air Force lined-up at Whitley before delivery to Norway early in 1936. Planned licence production of the Scimitar in Norway did not materialise.

The first Whitley prototype, K4586, at Whitley in 1936. Powered by two 795 hp supercharged Armstrong Siddeley Tiger IX engines driving three-blade two position de Havilland propellers, the Whitley was designed to meet Air Ministry specification B.3/34 for a 'heavy bomber landplane'.

AWA's chief test pilot Charles K. Turner-Hughes and his deputy, Eric S. Greenwood, in front of Whitley Mk.I K7194 at Baginton, in June 1937.

A line-up of four Whitley B.Is (K7203 to K7206 inclusive) at Baginton in September 1937, waiting for delivery to No. 78 Squadron at Dishforth. Early Whitleys had fairings fitted in place of the nose and tail gun turrets due to a shortage of turrets.

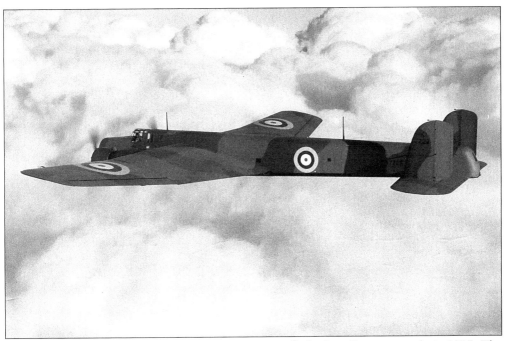

The sixth production Whitley B.II, K7222, on a test flight from Baginton early in 1938. The Whitley B.II differed from the Mk.I mainly by the introduction of the more powerful two speed supercharged Tiger VIII engines rated at 845 hp. This particular aircraft was delivered to No. 10 Squadron and subsequently served with Nos. 58 and 97 Squadrons before ending its days with No. 10 Operational Training Unit.

Whitley B.II, K7244, of No. 7 (B) Squadron in 1938. K7244 was written off when it ditched in Abersoch Bay on 19 February 1941 due to engine failure when being operated by No. 9 Bombing and Gunnery School (B&GS) at Penrhos.

Whitley B.II, K7243, used as the flying test bed for Armstrong Siddeley's 15-cylinder 3-row Deerhound engine. It is shown here with a new type of cowling designed to improve the cooling of the rear row of cylinders. K7243 flew for the first time with the Deerhound engines on 6 January 1939.

The Deerhound powered Whitley K7243 crashed on take-off from Baginton on 6 March 1940, killing all the Armstrong Siddeley flight test crew.

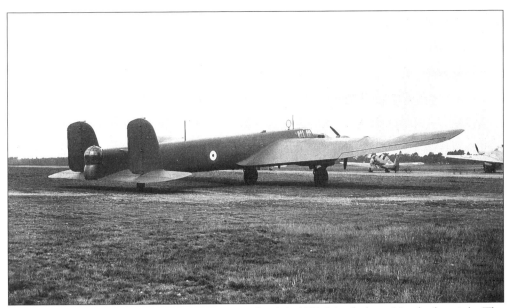

The first production Whitley B.III, K8936, at the A&AEE, Martlesham Heath, for trials. The main differences were the introduction of a Nash and Thompson FN16 power operated turret in the nose and an FN17 retractable 'dustbin' turret at the mid under station.

Whitley B.III final assembly at Baginton on 16 August 1938. The two Whitley B.Is bearing squadron markings have been returned to AWA for modification.

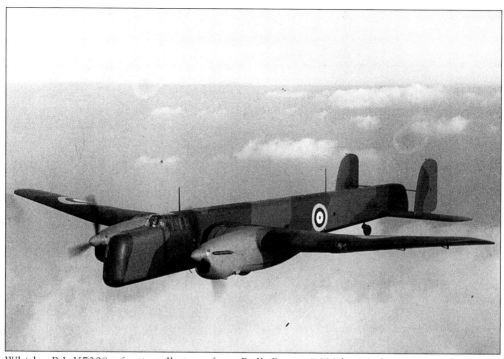

Whitley B.I, K7208, after installation of two Rolls Royce 1,030 hp Merlin IV engines, making it in effect the prototype Whitley B.IV.

Whitley B.IV, K9025, the tenth of 33 production B.IVs that were all built during 1939. K9025 was destroyed on 18 April 1942 when it crashed into a hangar at Kinloss following an engine failure on take-off.

N1345, the first production Whitley B.V, made its initial flight on 4 August 1939 with Eric S. Greenwood at the controls. The Whitley B.V was the most extensively produced variant of the Whitley with a total of 1,466 being produced. It differed from the B.IVA primarily in having a lengthened fuselage, redesigned fins and rubber de-icing boots on the wing leading edges.

The Prime Minister, Winston Churchill, accompanied by his wife on a visit to AWA's Baginton factory on 26 September 1941. The stripped airframe of SE5A, G-EBIA, that he is inspecting was placed alongside modern aircraft, in this case a Whitley bomber, so that visitors could see in a vivid manner the advances made in aviation since the First World War. The SE5A was stored by AWA for many years before it was donated to the Shuttleworth Trust, who, with the help of the RAE at Farnborough, returned it to flying condition.

The seventh production Whitley B.V, N1352, on a test flight from Baginton in 1939. It was lost during operations with No. 77 Squadron when it ditched in the North Sea returning from a shipping raid on Trondheim on 19 April 1940.

Whitley B.V, Z9226 of No. 10 Squadron. It was later transferred to No. 77 Squadron and was lost during a raid on Dusseldorf on 28 December 1941. The photograph clearly shows the nose down attitude of the Whitley when it was in level flight, caused by the angle of incidence of the wing.

Whitley B.V, G-AGDY (ex BD386), one of 15 converted to freighters for BOAC. The Whitleys soon proved unsuitable for the freighting role and were returned to the RAF in 1943.

Whitley GR.VII, LA794, one of 146 new build Mk.VIIs designed to meet the general reconnaissance role. This variant was readily identified by the array of aerials required for the Air to Surface Vessel(ASV) Mk.II radar. In addition to the aerials on top of the fuselage there were also aerials along the fuselage sides and under the nose and wings. LA794 ended its service as a flying classroom with the Royal Navy, being used to teach pilots the art of engine handling.

Whitley Mk.V, LA951, the last production Whitley, was retained by AWA as the glider tug for the AW52G flying wing glider. It was scrapped in June 1949, by which time it was almost certainly the last surviving Whitley of the 1,814 built.

The Sphinx Light Orchestra was inaugurated during the war by Herbert M. Woodhams, the managing director of AWA, to boost workers' morale by providing them with some light entertainment. The orchestra, under the leadership of Harry Wilson and with Reg Colston as conductor, provided lunchtime concerts in the canteens at Whitley and Baginton. In addition the orchestra gave concerts for the local community and particularly local military units.

The full scale mock-up of the Armstrong Whitworth AW41 Albemarle at Whitley in September 1938. It was obviously built to the initial design, which specified Rolls Royce Merlin engines. The Albemarle was designed to Air Ministry specification B.9/38 for a reconnaissance bomber that was to be constructed primarily out of wood and steel, in anticipation of a shortage of aluminium, and that with the exception of the final assembly, they would be built by companies outside the aircraft industry.

The first prototype AW41, Albemarle P1360, powered by two 1,590 hp Bristol Hercules XI air cooled 14-cylinder 2-row radial engines. Photographed at Hamble shortly after the first flight that had taken place on 20 March 1940, with AWA's chief test pilot Charles K. Turner-Hughes at the controls, it was destroyed when it crashed at Crewkerne, Somerset, on 4 February 1941 during trials at the A&AEE, Boscombe Down. Due to AWA's heavy commitment to Whitley production the two prototypes were built by Air Service Training Ltd at Hamble. Designed from the outset to have a tricycle undercarriage, it became the first aircraft with a tricycle undercarriage to be operated by the RAF.

The second production Albemarle B.I was retained by AWA for development purposes. The larger fins and rudders, along with the increased wingspan, were standard on all production Albemarles. These changes were also carried out retrospectively to the prototype to counter unsatisfactory flying characteristics.

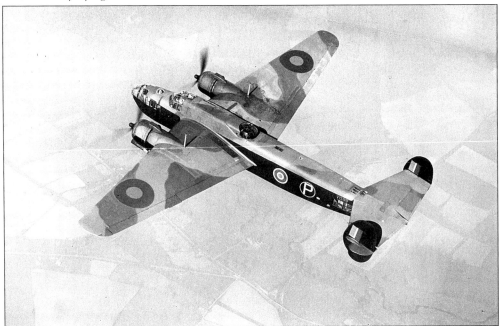

V1599, the last of 90 Albemarle GT.Is (glider tug), was retained by AWA to serve as the prototype ST.I special transport variant and then, in November 1943, was fitted with an experimental long-travel undercarriage.

An Albemarle on final assembly at Brockworth. All 600 production Albemarles were built at Brockworth, initially by the Gloster Aircraft Company and later by a new Hawker Siddeley Group company, A.W. Hawkesley Ltd, that was specifically set up to take over the manufacture of Albemarles at the Brockworth factory. Only the first 32 production Albemarles were built as reconnaissance bombers; all the later aircraft were glider tugs or special transports.

Albemarle ST.II, P1442. This variant was designed to carry ten paratroops forward of a dropping hatch in the floor of the rear fuselage.

The Albemarle GT.IV, P1406, was the single example of this variant which was powered by the American Wright Double Cyclone engine in place of the usual Bristol Hercules.

Albemarle ST.V, V1823, of No. 297 Squadron, having been painted with black and white invasion stripes. It crashed at Bretton on 22 December 1944 while towing a glider when serving with No. 22 HGCU.

One of 12 Albemarle ST.Is allocated to the USSR in 1944. This view clearly shows the sliding hood in place of the dorsal gun turret and the freight doors in the starboard side.

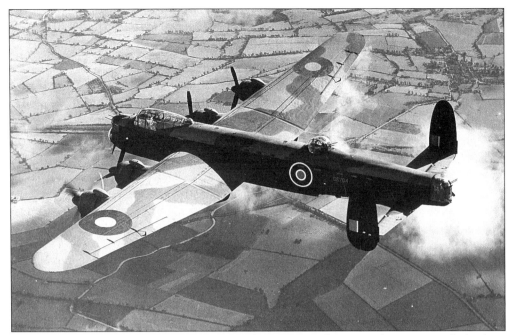

Lancaster B.II, DS704, demonstrating its single engine performance during a test flight from Baginton in the hands of C.K. Turner-Hughes on 27 August 1943. All 200 of the Bristol Hercules powered production Lancaster B.IIs were built by AWA.

The Lancaster B.I final assembly line at Bitteswell during 1944. LM396, which can be seen on the track, survived the war after completing 54 operations with No. 50 Squadron coded VN-T.

AWA's last production Lancaster B.I, TW911, was used as a flying test bed by Armstrong Siddeley Motors Ltd for their Python turbo-prop engine.

Douglas C.54B Skymaster I, EW999 (ex USAF 43-17126) at Baginton after being converted into a VIP transport for the personal use of Winston Churchill by AWA. Its first flight after conversion was made on 3 November 1944 with Charles Turner-Hughes at the controls, and two days later it was flown to Northolt for inspection by the Prime Minister.

A view of the conference room aboard EW999 with Churchill's chair at the head of the table.

A wind tunnel model of the AW52G glider in the low speed wind tunnel at Whitley in September 1943. The AW52G was designed to provide aerodynamic and control data for larger, powered flying wings that were planned by the company.

The AW52G under construction in the wood shop at AWA's Whitley factory in 1944. It was transferred to Baginton early in 1945 to be prepared for its first flight.

The AW52G with Ron Midgley, the chief test pilot, standing in front. His successor, Eric G. Franklin, is in the cockpit with W.W. Barratt, the flight test observer behind him.

The AW52G, RG324, on tow behind the last production Whitley B.V, LA951. The windmills mounted to the front of each main undercarriage leg were to provide boundary layer suction. The Whitley tug was replaced by Lancaster PA366 in December 1948. The AW52G completed its flight programme in 1950 and was subsequently put on display in the car park at Baginton. The company's plans to preserve RG324 came to nothing and it was scrapped in the late '50s.

Hurricane II, Z3687, alongside the AW52G in the flight shed at Baginton after AWA had fitted low drag wings as part of their research programme into boundary layer control. Its first flight with the new wings was at Baginton on 23 March 1945 in the hands of C.K. Turner-Hughes.

Z3687 during its only public appearance after receiving its all white paint scheme, in the static park at the SBAC show at Farnborough in September 1948.

A section of an aluminium prefabricated house built by AWA. At the end of the Second World War there was a serious housing shortage and this, coinciding with a large reduction in orders for military aircraft, resulted in the Government placing contracts with several of the aircraft companies for the production of prefabricated houses that were built primarily of aluminium alloy.

The AWA factory at Baginton shortly after the end of the Second World War. AWA started to move into the new factory at Baginton in 1936 and it remained the main production unit for the company until its closure in 1965, by which time the company had lost its original name and was operating as Hawker Siddeley Aviation.

Five
The Jet Age

Eric Franklin poses the Rolls Royce Nene powered TS363 for the cameras of the aeronautical press on 31 December 1947. Although serial numbers and the prototype (P) markings were carried, national markings were never applied to either of the two AW52s.

The remains of TS363 after it had crashed at Leamington Hastings on 30 May 1949 following a successful emergency evacuation of the aircraft by AWA test pilot J.O. Lancaster, using an early Martin Baker ejection seat. This gave Lancaster the rather dubious distinction of being the first pilot to have used an ejection seat to escape from an aircraft in an emergency.

The second AW52, TS368, powered by Rolls Royce Derwent engines, on an experimental flight from the RAE Farnborough. The dark areas are the test sections which were treated with chemicals that identified the line of demarcation between the turbulent and laminar flow areas.

AWA built Avro Lincoln B.II, RF570, operated by the Bomber Command Bombing School in 1959.

Lincoln B.II, RF574, showing damage received after nosing over on 9 April 1947 when it had taxied into soft ground on the grass airfield at Baginton.

Lincoln B.II, RF385, of No. 57 Squadron in the colour scheme of the Tiger Force for operation in the Far East. This aircraft crashed in Leicestershire on 20 February 1946.

One of the 18 Lincoln B.IIs built by AWA for the Argentinian Air Force, photographed in Argentina during June 1950.

Two Avro Yorks being prepared at Baginton on 17 November 1949 for return to service on the Berlin Airlift. It is claimed that at the peak of the overhaul programme, Yorks were being turned round in three days and during the period of the airlift, AWA overhauled 86.

John ('Jimmy') Lloyd was responsible for the design of all Siddeley Deasy and AWA aircraft and missiles. He had joined Siddeley Deasy in 1917 as chief designer and had continued in that role in AWA until 1948 when he was appointed technical director, a position he retained until his retirement in 1959.

The mock-up of the AW55 Apollo 24-passenger airliner that had been designed to meet the Brabazon IIB requirement. During the final years of the Second World War, the British Government had set up a committee under the chairmanship of Lord Brabazon to prepare specifications for civil transport aircraft that would be required by airlines following the end of the war. AWA received a contract to build two prototypes of their project to meet the Brabazon IIB specification.

The first prototype AW55 Apollo in final assembly at Baginton. Work on the construction of the prototype had started late in 1947 and the aircraft was completed in March 1949.

The AS Mamba turbo-prop powered prototype Apollo VX220, shown here on an early flight. It had made its maiden flight on 10 April 1949 with Eric Franklin at the controls and W.H. 'Bill' Else as second pilot.

In August 1950 the colour scheme of G-AIYN was again completely changed; it is seen here in the new scheme and with four-bladed propellers fitted to the inboard engines. The Apollo failed to achieve production status, being beaten by its competitor the Vickers VC2 Viscount that was to become one of Britain's most successful airliners.

Percival Proctor V, G-AHBD, on 5 March 1962. This aircraft served AWA as the company hack through the 1950s and into the first half of the 1960s.

Avro 19 Series 1 Anson G-AHYN, another of the AWA fleet of communications aircraft, at Baginton on 12 May 1953. At this time AWA operated three communications aircraft: the Proctor, Anson and a DH89 Dragon Rapide, G-AEML.

AWA's first production Gloster Meteor F.4, VZ386, at Baginton on 29 July 1949, having flown for the first time on 8 July 1949.

Meteor F.4s, 1412, the last of a batch of six built by AWA for the Royal Egyptian Air Force, at Baginton on 13 March 1950. This aircraft was delivered to the Gloster Aircraft Company at Moreton Valance on 30 March 1950 prior to delivery to Egypt.

A line-up of Meteor F.8s awaiting delivery at Baginton on 31 May 1950.

Two AWA built Meteor F.8s, WK914 and WH305, of No. 85 Squadron.

Meteor T.7, VW413, at Baginton in November 1949. This aircraft was converted by AWA at Baginton for use as an aerodynamic test aircraft for the Meteor night fighter development programme. The main changes are the extended nose to accommodate the airborne interception AI Mk.9C radar, the Gloster E1/44 type tail unit that was also used for the Meteor F.8 and the long span wings as fitted to the Meteor F.3.

The first prototype Meteor NF.11, WA546, at Baginton shortly before it made its maiden flight on 31 May 1950 with Eric G. Franklin at the controls. The failure of the AI Mk.9C radar resulted in the AI Mk.10 radar becoming standard for the production Meteor NF.11s. The blister fairing under the radome was to provide clearance for the scanner hinge.

Meteor NF.11s of No. 29 (F) Squadron as part of the fly past at the Queen's Review of the RAF at Odiham on 15 July 1953.

Meteor NF.11s of the French Air Force at Bitteswell on 4 February 1953, awaiting delivery to France. The French Air Force took delivery of a total of 25 new build Meteor NF.11s and 16 refurbished ex RAF aircraft.

Meteor NF.12s of No. 25 Squadron on a visit to AWA at Bitteswell on 30 April 1954. The Meteor NF.12 differed from the NF Mk.11 in having a longer nose to house the American AI Mk.21 (APS 57) radar, and the increased fin area.

A Meteor NF.13, WM321, of No. 219 Squadron based at Kabrit in Egypt. The Meteor NF.13 is basically a tropicalised NF.11, having been fitted with an air conditioning unit in the cockpit.

Meteor NF.11, WM261, after conversion to become the prototype Meteor NF.14, on 29 July 1953 before the completion of its paint scheme.

Meteor NF.14s of No. 85 Squadron on a visit to AWA at Bitteswell on 24 May 1954. The Meteor NF.14 is similar to the NF.12 except that it is fitted with the large clear view cockpit canopies.

The first Meteor TT.20 conversion, WD767, reels out its sleeve target during a test flight on 16 April 1958. When in use for actual target practise the sleeve target could be up to 6,100 ft behind the aircraft. WD767 was retained by the company for development purposes.

Meteor TT.20, 51-508, of the Royal Danish Air Force, one of the six that were converted by AWA from their existing fleet of Meteor NF.11s.

The Meteor F.8, WK935, being converted at Baginton in September 1953 for prone pilot research to provide data for the RAF Institute of Aviation Medicine at Farnborough.

Prone pilot Meteor WK935 during a test flight on 1 July 1954. When flown by the pilot in the prone position there was always a pilot in the conventional cockpit for safety purposes. This interesting aircraft is preserved in the Aerospace Museum at RAF Cosford.

Design and production facilities at the Hawker factories were put under considerable pressure when both their Sea Hawk and Hunter fighters were given super priority status for the Royal Navy and Royal Air Force respectively. Consequently, in 1952 the responsibility for design and production of the Sea Hawk was transferred to AWA. The photograph shows final assembly of Sea Hawk F.1s at Bitteswell in October 1953. AWA's first production Sea Hawk, WF162, had made its first flight on 18 December 1952, with their chief test pilot Eric Franklin at the controls.

Sea Hawk F.1, WF181/174, of No. 806 Squadron, Fleet Air Arm, taxying on board HMS Eagle in 1954. No. 806 Squadron was the first front line squadron to be equipped with Sea Hawks. It reformed with Sea Hawks at RNAS Brawdy on 2 March 1953 and embarked on HMS Eagle on 1 February 1954.

The first Sea Hawk F.2, WF240, seen here at Bitteswell on 14 April 1955, was retained by AWA for development purposes. To correct a problem of lateral control that existed on the F.1, the F.2 introduced fully powered aileron control with spring feel.

The Sea Hawk FB.3 had strengthened wings to enable it to undertake the fighter bomber role. WF280, the first FB.3, is shown here at Bitteswell on 14 April 1955 carrying four bombs. A number of the FB.3s were subsequently converted to FB.5s by the introduction of a more powerful version of the Rolls Royce Nene engine.

The Sea Hawk FGA.4 was the first definitive ground attack variant with strengthened outer wings to allow the carriage of rocket projectiles and bombs. WV840 - still bearing the markings of 802 Squadron, a previous operator of the aircraft - is seen here with special underwing tanks fitted with flight refuelling probes for air-to-air refuelling trials using a Canberra tanker at Flight Refuelling Ltd.

The availability of an up-rated Rolls Royce Nene 103 engine saw the Sea Hawk FGA.4 being superseded on the production line by the FGA.6. In addition a number of FGA.4s were converted to FGA.6s by retrofitting the new engine. Sea Hawk FGA.6, XE456, is seen here with an assortment of underwing stores in readiness for display at the SBAC Exhibition at Farnborough in September 1956.

The Sidewinder armed Sea Hawk FGA.50, 6-66 of No. 3 Training Squadron, Royal Netherlands Navy, Valkenburg. The Netherlands' Sea Hawk fleet was retrospectively modified to carry the Sidewinder 1A air-to-air guided missile as its primary defensive armament.

Sea Hawk FGA6s of 804 and 800 Squadrons, along with de Havilland Sea Venom F(AW).21s of 893 Squadron on board HMS Ark Royal, on deployment to the Mediterranean early in 1958.

Three West German Navy Sea Hawk Mk.100s during a flight from Bitteswell on 28 March 1958. Note the large fin and rudder that is the main external change from the Royal Navy Sea Hawks.

AWA test pilots, W.H. Else, E.G. Franklin and J.G. McCowan, just before setting out on the delivery flights of Sea Hawks VA232, VA233 and VA234 to Bremen on 2 June 1958.

The last production German Sea Hawk Mk.101, RB376, at Bitteswell on 2 April 1959. This version was designed to carry Ecko search radar installed in a special pod that was mounted on the inner starboard pylon.

Sea Hawk FGA.6, IN151 of the Indian Navy at Bitteswell on 19 January 1960. This aircraft (ex WF301) was the first of a batch of ex Royal Navy Sea Hawk FB.3s that were converted to FGA.6s for the Indian Navy by AWA.

A view inside No. 2 Hangar at New Site, Bitteswell. In addition to the Meteor and Sea Hawk development aircraft there is Vickers Valetta VL264, which although allotted to the Telecommunications Research Establishment (TRE) at Defford, was used for various trials of Meteor avionics by AWA between 1950 and 1955.

The first AWA built Armstrong Siddeley Sapphire powered Hunter F.2, WN888, at Bitteswell in November 1953. Appropriately AWA was responsible for the production of all the Sapphire powered Hunters, both F.2s and F.5s. The Hunter F.2 was the equivalent of the Rolls Royce Avon powered Hunter F.1.

A line-up of seven Hunter F.5s, including WN964 and WN968, at Bitteswell on 7 December 1954.

The final variant of the Hunter to be built by AWA was the Rolls Royce Avon powered Hunter F.6. This photograph shows an AWA built Hunter F.6, XF389, carrying two 100 gallon drop tanks and 24 rocket projectiles.

The full scale mock-up of the AW168 project at Whitley in January 1955. It was abandoned when the Ministry of Supply selected the competing Blackburn project, which was to see service with both the Royal Navy and RAF as the Buccaneer.

AWA's second production Javelin F(AW).4, XA721, being marshalled in at Bitteswell at the end of a test flight. The Javelin F(AW).4 was the first Javelin to have an all-moving tailplane.

Javelin F(AW).5, XA667, shortly after AWA test pilot Martin Walton had made a successful emergency landing sustaining only superficial damage to the radome when the nosewheel jammed in the retracted position.

Javelin F(AW).9, XH897, was built as an F(AW).7 by AWA. After service with Nos. 5, 25 and 33 Squadrons as an F(AW).7, it was converted to an F(AW).9 and then used by the A&AEE at Boscombe Down for position error correction and flight calibration duties. It remained in service with the A&AEE until January 1975, when it joined the Imperial Museum Collection at Duxford.

A model of the four engined AW169 interceptor fighter which was to have had Red Dean missiles as the primary armament. The AWA and Fairey projects were selected to proceed to the development phase, but both were cancelled following the 1957 Defence White Paper which decreed no more manned fighters for the RAF.

The AW650 Argosy full scale mock-up, built of wood with an aluminium skin at Baginton in May 1957. The Ministry of Supply had withdrawn its support for a military freighter in 1956 because of a shortage of funds. However AWA, with the support of the Hawker Siddeley Group, continued with a civilian freighter variant of the project as a private venture.

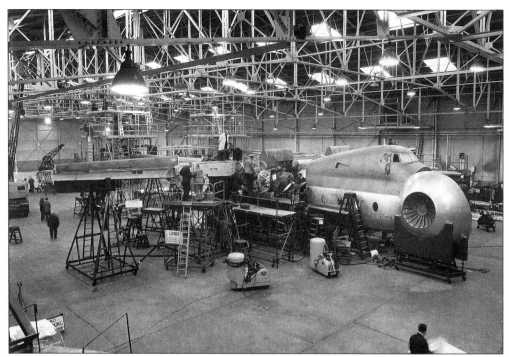

The first Argosy, G-AOZZ, being assembled at Bitteswell Old Site in October 1958, showing very clearly the hinged nose section. Hawker Siddeley authorised an initial production batch of ten Argosy Series 100 aircraft.

G-AOZZ during a test flight on 23 February 1959, having made its maiden flight shortly before on 8 January 1959.

Argosy Series 102, N6505R, of Riddle Airlines Inc. of Miami, Florida, at Tinker Air Force Base, Oklahoma. This view shows how it can be unloaded through the nose whilst being loaded through the rear. Riddle Airlines was the biggest civil operator of the Argosy, operating five of their fleet of seven on the USAF Military Air Transport Service (MATS) Logistics Air Support System (LOGAIR) service. LOGAIR was a very intensive delivery service for equipment between USAF air bases.

Bitteswell Aerodrome on 8 May 1962, with the Old Site in the foreground and New Site in the distance. After Baginton and Whitley had closed in the mid 1960s, Bitteswell continued until it also succumbed to the continuing contraction of the aircraft industry, closing in 1985.

The first Argosy 200, G-ASKZ, at Bitteswell New Site prior to introduction of wing fences to improve stall handling characteristics. This aircraft was used by AWA for development and was scrapped in 1967 when the company was unable to find a customer.

G-ASXO was the fourth Argosy Series 222, delivered to BEA on 28 April 1965. It was later sold to Transair Midwest Airlines of Canada in 1970 where it was registered CF-TAX. BEA proved to be the only customer for the later Argosy, ordering five Series 222 in 1964 and later a further one as a replacement for one that had crashed in Italy. The three that were not sold remained incomplete and after being mothballed for several years were scrapped.

Safe Air Argosy Series 222, ZK-SAE named *Merchant Enterprise*. It is believed that after 17 years of service in New Zealand this particular aircraft is being preserved.

Production of Argosy C.1 fuselages at the Baginton factory in January 1961. A total of 56 Argosies were built for the RAF.

Argosy C.1s, XN821 and XN850, of No. 114 Squadron. Based at Benson, 114 was the first squadron to be equipped with the Argosy. The nose radome accommodated the weather radar scanner.

A model of the Bristol Siddeley Pegasus powered AW681 STOL Transport project. Rolls Royce Medway engines were subsequently selected for the development phase of the programme but in 1965 the Government cancelled the project, which led directly to the closure of the Baginton factory.